DIRTY LINEN
and
NEW-FOUND-LAND

Other Works by Tom Stoppard
Published by Grove Press

DIRTY LINEN
and
NEW-FOUND-LAND

TOM STOPPARD

GROVE PRESS, INC., NEW YORK

ISBN: 0-394-41179-X
Grove Press ISBN: 0-8021-0130-5

Library of Congress Catalog Card Number: 76-45521

First Edition 1976

First Printing

Manufactured in the United States of America

Distributed by Random House, Inc., New York

GROVE PRESS, INC., 196 West Houston Street, New York, N.Y. 10014

To Ed Berman

The first performances of *Dirty Linen* and *New-Found-Land* were an Ambiance Lunch-Hour Theatre Club presentation at Inter-Action's Almost Free Theatre, Rupert Street, London W1, on 6th April 1976. The cast was as follows:

Dirty Linen

MADDIE	Luan Peters
COCKLEBURY-SMYTHE, M.P.	Edward de Souza
MCTEAZLE, M.P.	Benjamin Whitrow
CHAMBERLAIN, M.P.	Malcolm Ingram
WITHENSHAW, M.P. (the CHAIRMAN)	Peter Bowles
MRS. EBURY, M.P.	Christine Ozanne
FRENCH, M.P.	Richard O'Callaghan
HOME SECRETARY	Derek Ensor

New-Found-Land

ARTHUR	Stephen Moore
BERNARD	Richard Goolden

Directed by Ed Berman
Designed by Gabriella Falk
Production Management and lighting by Suresa Galbraith
Administration by Martin Turner
Stage Management by Robin Hornibrook and Brenda Lipson
Wardrobe by Carol Betera

The plays transferred to the Arts Theatre on 16th June 1976 with the following cast changes:

MCTEAZLE, M.P.	Frederick Treves
FRENCH, M.P.	Jonathan Elsom

DIRTY LINEN

A play in one act

Characters

MADDIE
COCKLEBURY-SMYTHE, M.P.
MCTEAZLE, M.P.
CHAMBERLAIN, M.P.
WITHENSHAW, M.P. (the CHAIRMAN)
MRS. EBURY, M.P.
FRENCH, M.P.
HOME SECRETARY

An overspill meeting room for House of Commons business in the tower of Big Ben. A committee table with chairs for everybody; separate table with good slammable drawers for MADDIE; *large blackboard on easel; shelves of files and books, with portable steps; and two doors.*

Ultimately the characters will be seated in the following order, left to right from the audience's point of view: FRENCH, CHAMBERLAIN, COCKLEBURY-SMYTHE, WITHENSHAW (*centre*), MRS. EBURY, MCTEAZLE, *and* MADDIE *at separate desk.*

The room is empty. MADDIE *puts her head round the door cautiously, enters in street coat and carrying a small classy looking bag from a classy lingerie shop, and a handbag. The room is unfamiliar to her. She hangs up her coat on a coat/hat/umbrella stand which is just inside the door, walks to the desk, and after a moment's hesitation she takes a pair of silk, lace-trimmed French knickers out of the bag and puts them on.*

MADDIE *finishes putting on her knickers and drops her skirt. The knickers ought to be remembered for their colour—perhaps white silk with red lace trimmings.*

MADDIE *is now wearing a low cut, sleeveless blouse, buttoned insecurely down the front; a wrap-round skirt, quite short; underneath, suspenders not tights, and a waist-slip which is also pretty, silk and lace, with a slit.*

From her bag she takes a notebook and a pencil and puts them on the desk. There are glasses and a carafe on the large table. She picks up the lingerie bag and looks around for a waste-paper basket. Finding none, she leaves by the other door, bag in hand. The first door is now opened by MCTEAZLE *who holds it open for* COCKLEBURY-SMYTHE.

COCKLEBURY-SMYTHE (*entering*): Toujours la politesse.
MCTEAZLE (*closing the door*): Noblesse oblige.

(*They each carry several newspapers, a whole crop of the day's papers and the Sundays, which they dump on the big table. They doff their bowler hats and attempt to put them on the same peg.*)

Mea culpa. (*Courteously.*)

COCKLEBURY-SMYTHE: Après vous.

(MCTEAZLE *signals that* COCKLEBURY-SMYTHE *should hang up his hat first. They put their brollies in the umbrella stand.* COCKLEBURY-SMYTHE *sits down.*)

J'y suis, j'y reste. (*He opens the* Daily Mail.) Quel dommage.

MCTEAZLE (*sitting down*): Le mot juste.

COCKLEBURY-SMYTHE: C'est la vie. Che sera sera. (*He throws the paper aside.*)

(MCTEAZLE *picks up the* Daily Mirror *and turns to page 3 which features a glamour picture, not particularly revealing.*)

MCTEAZLE: Ooh la-la! (*Then he recovers his dignity. Deprecatingly.*) Vox populi . . . plus ça change, plus c'est la même chose. (*He throws the paper aside and picks up the* Guardian.)

COCKLEBURY-SMYTHE: De gustibus non est disputandum.

(*Pause.*)

MCTEAZLE (*hesitantly*): A propos . . . entre nous . . . vis-à-vis le Coq d'Or.

COCKLEBURY-SMYTHE: Ah, le Coq d'Or . . .

MCTEAZLE: Faux pas, hein?

COCKLEBURY-SMYTHE: Bloody awkward though. Pardon my French.

(MADDIE *re-enters with a waste-paper basket.* MCTEAZLE *does not see her as he is engrossed in the* Guardian. COCKLEBURY-SMYTHE *sees her but registers nothing.*)

Honi soit qui mal y pense.

(*On which, without pausing, he produces from an inside pocket a pair of French knickers and hands them to* MADDIE *as she crosses to her desk collecting them urbanely.*)

Ergo nil desperandum.

(COCKLEBURY-SMYTHE *picks up his copy of the* Daily Mirror *and turns to the pin-up on page 3. He makes a wordless noise appropriate to male approval of female pulchritude. This coincides with* MADDIE *bending over, showing cleavage, to put*

*the knickers into a drawer of her desk. This moment of the man
reacting to the pin-up photograph, and the coincidental image
of* MADDIE *in a pin-up pose is something which is to be repeated
several times, so for brevity's sake it will be hereafter
symbolized by the expletive 'Strewth!' It must be marked
distinctly; a momentary freeze on stage, and probably a flash
of light like a camera flash.* MADDIE *should look straight out at
the audience for that moment.*)

Strewth!

(*After the freeze* MCTEAZLE *sees* MADDIE.)

MCTEAZLE: Good afternoon. (*He stands up.*) I am Mr. McTeazle
and you are . . . ?

MADDIE: Miss Gotobed.

MCTEAZLE: Miss Gotobed. And this is Mr. Cocklebury-Smythe.

COCKLEBURY-SMYTHE: How do you do?

MADDIE: Hello.

COCKLEBURY-SMYTHE: So you are going to be our clerk.

MADDIE: Yes.

COCKLEBURY-SMYTHE: May I be the first to welcome you to
Room 3b. You will find the working conditions primitive,
the hours antisocial, the amenities non-existent and the
catering beneath contempt. On top of that the people are for
the most part very very very boring, with interests either so
generalized as to mimic wholesale ignorance or so particular
as to be lunatic obsessions. Their level of conversation
would pass without comment in the lavatory of a mixed
comprehensive and the lavatories, by the way, are few and
far between.

MADDIE: It has always been my ambition to work in the House
of Commons.

(*Sound of Big Ben chiming the half hour.*)

COCKLEBURY-SMYTHE: Mine has always been the House of Lords.
But then perhaps I have not been willing to make the same
sacrifices you have.

MCTEAZLE: Have you had to make sacrifices Miss Gotobed? Not
too arduous I hope?

MADDIE: It was hard work but I enjoyed the challenge.

COCKLEBURY-SMYTHE (*quickly*): Yes . . . yes, the P.M. offered me a life peerage, for services which he said he would let me know more about in due course if I were interested. 'I hear you're a keen gardener, Cockie,' he said, 'we can call it services to conservation.' 'Not me, Rollo,' I said, 'all I use it for is a little topiary in the summer.' 'Services to sport,' he said, 'ignorant fool.' 'No, no, Rollo,' I said, 'I really have no interests of any kind.' 'That will be services to the arts,' he said. 'Stop making such a fuss—do you want a life peerage or don't you?' 'No I don't,' I said to him. 'What with only a couple of bachelor cousins in line ahead, one of whom is an amateur parachutist and the other a seamstress in the Merchant Navy, I prefer to hang on for a chance of the real thing.' He said to me: 'My dear Cockie, life peers *are* the real thing nowadays.' 'Oh no they're not, Rollo,' I said. 'That's just the kind of confusion you set up in people's minds by calling them Lord This and Lord That, pour encourager hoi polloi. *They* think they're lords—they skip off home and feed the budgerigar saying to themselves, my golly gorblimey, I'm a lord! They'd be just as happy if you suddenly told them they were all sheiks. They'd put the *Desert Song* on the gramophone and clap their hands when they wanted their cocoa. Now *you'd* know they're not really sheiks and I'd know they're not really sheiks, and God help them if they ever showed up east of Suez in their appalling pullovers with Sheik Shuttleworth stencilled on their airline bags—no, my dear Rollo,' I said, 'I'll be a real peer or not at all.' 'Now look here, Cockie,' he said to me, 'if they weren't real peers they wouldn't be in the House of Lords would they?—that's logic.' 'If that's logic,' I said, 'you can turn a regimental goat into a Lieutenant Colonel by electing it to the United Services Club.' 'That's an interesting point, Cockie,' he said. 'It could explain a lot of my problems.' Do you suppose we've got the wrong day? (*He takes out a pocket diary and consults it.*) Oh yes— Select Committee, House of Commons—take L.P. . . . take L.P. . . . ? What L.P.?

MADDIE: It is the right day. I didn't get a wink of sleep all last night.

COCKLEBURY-SMYTHE (*mutters*): L.P. . . .

MADDIE: It's not every girl who gets advancement from the Home Office typing pool.

MCTEAZLE: I expect it's not every girl who proves herself as you have done, Miss Gotobed. Do you use Gregg's or do you favour the Pitman method?

MADDIE: I'm on the pill.

(*Small pause.* MCTEAZLE *is expressionless.*)

MCTEAZLE: Perhaps this might be an opportunity for me to explain to you the nature of the duties expected of a secretary/clerk attached to a Select Committee, duties which for one reason or another you may have got confused in your mind.

COCKLEBURY-SMYTHE (*suddenly*): Lace panties. Sorry.

MCTEAZLE: Now, this is a meeting of a Select Committee of Members of Parliament to report on moral standards in the House—not in the House literally, or rather, in the House literally but also, and for the most part, outside the House too.

MADDIE: In the car park?

MCTEAZLE: Not literally in the car park—or rather in the car park too, yes, but also—don't try to take in more than you can. Now, this is a continuation of a Select Committee set up during the last session of Parliament, though at that time the membership of the Committee was different. A Select Committee must be reconvened with each new session of Parliament, and it is this reconstituted Committee which is about to begin sitting to report on rumours of sexual promiscuity by certain unspecified Members which, if substantiated, might tend to bring into disrepute the House of Commons and possibly the Lords and one or two government departments including Social Security, Environment, Defence, Health, Agriculture and even, I'm sorry to say, the Milk Marketing Board.

MADDIE: Why's that?

MCTEAZLE: Because I have the honour to be on that Board and I think I can say without fear of contradiction that the M.M.B. has an unrivalled record of freedom from suggestions of

19

being a sexual free-for-all, and furthermore we are now
getting yoghurt and single and double cream to every
corner of——

MADDIE: Actually what I meant was, why would it bring them
into disrepute?

MCTEAZLE: Because the country by and large looks to its elected
representatives to set a moral standard . . .

MADDIE: No it doesn't——

MCTEAZLE (*smoothly*): No it doesn't—you're quite right. Then
it's because the authority of the—er—authorities is under-
mined by losing the respect of——

MADDIE: I don't think people care.

MCTEAZLE: No, people don't care—of course they don't. In which
case I think it is fair to say that this Committee owes its
existence to the determination of the Prime Minister to keep
his House in order, whatever the cost in public ridicule,
whatever the consequence to people in high places, and to
the fact that the newspapers got wind of what was going on.
It is unfortunate that the well known restraint and sense of
higher purpose which characterizes the British press—a
restraint which would have treated with utter contempt
stories of garter-snapping by a few M.P.s—gave way
completely at the rumour that they were all snapping the
same garter. You may know, if you are a student of the
press, or if you have at any time in the last few weeks
passed within six feet of a newspaper, that there is no phrase
as certain to make a British sub-editor lose his sense of
proportion as the phrase 'Mystery Woman'. This Committee
was set up at the time when the good name of no fewer than
21 Members of Parliament was said to have been com-
promised. Since then rumour has fed on rumour and we
face the possibility that a sexual swathe has passed through
Westminster claiming the reputations of, to put no finer
point upon it, 119 Members. Someone is going through the
ranks like a lawn-mower in knickers. Well, I need hardly
say—(*he is taking papers out of his brief case*)—that we as a
Committee are working in a sensitive area, one which
demands great tact on all our parts—(MCTEAZLE *produces*

20

from his brief case a pair of knickers and hands them to
MADDIE)—your own not excluded.
(MADDIE *collects the knickers urbanely and puts them in her knicker drawer; she has changed her position however and has to practically sprawl across the desk to do this, thus showing leg as well as cleavage. Simultaneously* COCKLEBURY-SMYTHE *has discovered a pin-up picture in the* Daily Mail, *or any other appropriate paper except the* Sun.)

COCKLEBURY-SMYTHE: Strewth!
(*After the freeze there seems to be nothing to occupy the two men.* MADDIE *collects herself and sits demurely on her desk. The two men get up and move around.*)
Well, this is getting us nowhere. Where is everybody?
(*In the following section, the italicized words are said privately to* MADDIE *with no change of tone or volume while the other is at the extreme of his perambulation.*)
Are we going to have a quorum? You may not be familiar with the term quorum incidentally *if anyone asks you where you had dinner last night* it's a Latin word meaning 'of which or of whom'. . . .

MCTEAZLE: Quite simply, it's the smallest number of members of a committee necessary to constitute the said committee, for example, say you were *nowhere near the Coq d'Or on Saturday night* then the smallest number of members without which a quorum can't be said to be a quorum——

COCKLEBURY-SMYTHE: A quorum is nothing more or less than the largest minimum specified number of members being that proportion of the whole committee, let us say three or four *get Coq d'Or Sunday night completely* invalid without them. Got it?

MCTEAZLE: It's not as complicated as it sounds.

MADDIE: Is it a specified number of members of a committee whose presence—God bless them—is necessary for the valid transaction of business by that committee?

MCTEAZLE: Yes . . . yes, that is pretty well what a quorum is. I can see, Miss Gotobed, that there is more to you than your name suggests—by which I mean (*trying to accelerate out of trouble*) that you don't spend all your time flat on your back

21

—or your front—your side, flat on your side, sleeping, fast asleep, when you could be doing your homework instead of living up to your name, which you don't, that's my point. (COCKLEBURY-SMYTHE *has been standing like stone, his glazed eyes absently fixed on* MADDIE's *cleavage.*)

COCKLEBURY-SMYTHE: McTeazle, why don't you go and see if you can raise those great tits—boobs—those boobies, absolute tits, don't you agree, Malcolm and Douglas—though good men as well, of course, useful chaps, very decent, first rate, two of the best, Malcolm and Douglas, why don't you have a quick poke, peek, in the Members' Bra—or the cafeteria, they're probably guzzling coffee and Swedish panties, (MADDIE *has crossed her legs*) Danish, I'll tell you what, why don't you go and see if you can raise Malcolm and Douglas—(*to* MADDIE)—sometimes there are more of these committees trying to meet than there are rooms for them to meet in—that's why we're up here in the tower instead of one of those nice rooms on the Committee Floor with the green leather chairs, though I expect you've spent a lot of time on the Floor, Miss Gotobed, by which I mean, of course, the Committee Bed, Floor—(*getting hysterical*)— McTeazle the Division Bell will go before we even get started and then we'll all have to go off and vote on some beastly amendment to make anyone who buys his own council house a life bishop with the right to wear a nightie on his head, mitre on his head. My God, I could do with a drink——

MCTEAZLE: You go then. No, I'll go. I'll tell you what, Miss Gotobed, why don't you come with me, I'll show you round the lavatories, round the House, show you the Chamber, the lavatories——

COCKLEBURY-SMYTHE: She doesn't want to go trudging round the House inspecting the toilets like a deputation from the Water Board. Let the poor girl alone—she didn't get a wink of sleep all night.

(*He ushers* MCTEAZLE *out and closes the door. He turns and addresses* MADDIE *immediately. In the following speech the italicized words coincide with* MCTEAZLE's *brief re-appearance to*

22

take his bowler hat off the hatstand.)

Maddie my dear, you look even more ravishing this
morning than *the smallest specified number of members of that
committee of which* we will have to be very very careful—it
is a cruel irony that our carefree little friendship, which
is as innocent and pure as the first driven snowdrop of
spring, is in danger of being trampled by the hobnailed
hue-and-cry over these absurd rumours of unbuttoned
behaviour in and out of both trousers of Parliament—I think
I can say, and say with confidence, that when the smoke has
cleared from the Augean stables, the little flame of our love
will still be something no one else can hold a candle to so
long as we can keep our heads down. In other words, my
darling girl, if anyone were to ask you where you had
lunch on Friday, breakfast on Saturday or dinner on
Sunday, best thing is to forget Crockford's, Claridges and
the Coq d'Or.

MADDIE (*concentrating*): Crockford's—Claridges—the Coq d'Or.

COCKLEBURY-SMYTHE: Forget—forget.

MADDIE: Forget. Forget Crockford's, Claridges, Coq d'Or.
Forget Crockford's, Claridges, Coq d'Or. (*To herself.*)
Forget Crockford's, Claridges, Coq d'Or. Forget Crock-
ford's, Claridges, Coq d'Or.

(COCKLEBURY-SMYTHE *sees that this is achieving the opposite.*)

COCKLEBURY-SMYTHE: All right—tell you what—say you had
breakfast at Claridges, *lunch* at the Coq d'Or, and had
dinner at Crockford's. Meanwhile I'll stick to——

MADDIE (*concentrating harder than ever*): Claridges, Coq d'Or,
Crockford's. Forget Crockford's, Claridges, Coq d'Or.
Remember Claridges, Coq d'Or, Crockford's. Remember
Claridges, Coq d'Or, Crockford's. Claridges, Coq d'Or,
Crockford's, Claridges, Coq d'Or, Crockford's.

COCKLEBURY-SMYTHE: But not with me.

MADDIE: Not with you. Not with Cockie at Claridges, Coq d'Or,
Crockford's. Never at Claridges, Coq d'Or, Crockford's
with Cockie. Never at Claridges, Coq d'Or, Crockford's
with Cockie.

(*Her concentration doesn't imply slowness: she is fast, eager,*

*breathless, very good at tongue twisters. Her whole attitude in
the play is one of innocent, eager willingness to please.*
COCKLEBURY-SMYTHE *sees that he is going about this the wrong
way.*)

COCKLEBURY-SMYTHE: Wait a minute. (*Rapidly.*) The best thing
is forget Claridges, Crockford's and the Coq d'Or altogether.

MADDIE: Right. Forget Claridges, Crockford's, Coq d'Or—
forget Claridges, Crockford's, Coq d'Or——

COCKLEBURY-SMYTHE: And if anyone asks you where you had
lunch on Friday, breakfast on Saturday and dinner last
night, when you were with me, tell them where you had
dinner on Friday, lunch on Saturday and breakfast
yesterday.

MADDIE: Right! (*Pause. She closes her eyes with concentration.*)
(*Rapidly.*) The Green Cockatoo, the Crooked Clock, the
Crock of Gold—and Box Hill.

COCKLEBURY-SMYTHE: Box Hill?

MADDIE: To see the moon come up—forget Crockford's,
Claridges, Coq d'Or—remember the Crock of Gold, Box
Hill, the Crooked Clock and the Green Door——

COCKLEBURY-SMYTHE: Cockatoo——

MADDIE: Cockatoo. Crock of Gold, Crooked Clock, Green
Cockatoo and Box Hill. When was this?

COCKLEBURY-SMYTHE: When you were really with me.

MADDIE: Right. With Cockie at the Green Cockatoo——

COCKLEBURY-SMYTHE: No *not* with Cockie at the Green Cockatoo.

MADDIE: —not with Cockie at the Green Cockatoo, the Old
Cook, the Crooked Grin, Gamages and Box Hill.

COCKLEBURY-SMYTHE (*wildly*): No—look. The simplest thing is to
forget, Claridges, the Old Boot, the Golden *quorum can be
any number agreed upon by*——
(*This is because* MCTEAZLE *is back.*)

MCTEAZLE: Douglas is on his way back. (*Hanging up his hat.*)

COCKLEBURY-SMYTHE: I've got to have a drink.
(*He leaves, forgetting his bowler hat, as* MCTEAZLE *closes the
door.* MCTEAZLE *starts speaking at once. The italicized words
correspond to* COCKLEBURY-SMYTHE's *momentary reappearances,
in the first case to take a bowler hat off the hatstand and in*

the second case to change hats because he has taken out
MCTEAZLE's *hat the first time.*)

MCTEAZLE: Maddie*ning the way one is kept waiting for* ours is a
very tricky position, my dear. In normal times one can
count on chaps being quite sympathetic to the sight of a
Member of Parliament having dinner with a lovely young
woman in some out-of-the-way nook—it could be a case of
constituency business, they're not necessarily screw-*oo-ooge
is, I think you'll find, not in 'David Copperfield' at all, still
less in 'The Old Curiosity Sho*'-cking though it is, the sight
of a Member of Parliament having some out-of-the-way
nookie with a lovely young woman might well be a case of a
genuine love match destined to take root and pass through
ever more respectable stages—the first shy tentative dinner
party in a basement flat in Pembridge Crescent for a few
trusted friends—Caxton Hall—and a real friendship with
the stepchildren—people are normally inclined to give one
the benefit of the doubt. But the tragedy is, as our luck
would have it, that our gemlike love which burns so true
and pure and has brought such a golden light into our
lives, could well become confused with a network of grubby
affairs between men who should know better and some bit
of fluff from the filing department—so I suggest, my darling,
if any one were to enquire where you may or may not have
spent Friday night or indeed Saturday lunch time or Sunday
tea time, forget Charing Cross, the Coq d'Or and the
Golden Ox.

MADDIE: Charing Cross, Coq d'Or, Golden Ox. Charing Cross,
Coq d'Or, Golden Ox. Charing Cross, Old Door, and the
Golden Cock——

MCTEAZLE:—Ox——

MADDIE: Ox.

MCTEAZLE: The Coq d'Or and the Golden Ox. Not the Golden
Cock and the Old Door.

MADDIE: Not the Golden Cock and the Old Door but the
Golden Ox and the Coq d'Or.

MCTEAZLE: And don't forget: Charing Cross.

MADDIE: Don't forget Charing Cross.

MCTEAZLE: I mean *forget* Charing Cross.

MADDIE: Forget Charing Cross——

MCTEAZLE: Plucky girl——

MADDIE: Plucky girl—Charing Cross—Olden cocks.

MCTEAZLE: But not with me.

MADDIE: Not with Jock at the Old Cock——

MCTEAZLE: Door. (*This is because the door has opened.*)

MADDIE: Old Coq d'Or—not with Jock.

(CHAMBERLAIN *has entered.*)

MCTEAZLE (*hurriedly*): Hello, Douglas.

(CHAMBERLAIN *is repellently full of zest and heartiness. He also carries an armful of papers which he dumps on the table. He treats* MADDIE *with open, crude lechery.*)

CHAMBERLAIN: Hello!

MCTEAZLE: This is Mr. Chamberlain. Miss Gotobed is going to be our clerk.

(CHAMBERLAIN *advances on* MADDIE *who backs off behind her desk and starts opening drawers to look busy.*)

CHAMBERLAIN: What?!—that luscious creature is our clerk! Impossible! Where's her moustache? Her dandruff? Her striped pants?

(MADDIE *reflexively slams shut her knicker drawer.*)

What an uncommonly comely clerk you are! My name's Douglas. I hope you don't mind me saying that you're a lovely girl—I don't mind telling you that if I wasn't married to a wonderful girl myself with two fine youngsters down in Dorking and an au pair to complicate my life, I'd be after you and no mistake,

(*During the rest of this speech,* MADDIE *pushes past* CHAMBERLAIN, *goes over to her coat and takes a copy of the* Sun *from her pocket. She returns towards her desk.*)

my goodness yes, it would be private coaching in a little French restaurant somewhere, a few hints on parliamentary procedure over the boeuf bourgignon, and then off in the Volvo while I mutter sweet definitions in your ear and test your elastic with the moon coming up over Box Hill.

(*As* MADDIE *passes the steps, he gooses her so thoroughly that she goes straight up them, still holding the* Sun. CHAMBERLAIN

26

slaps a sheet of paper on her desk.)
Have you an order of business? (*He turns aside.*) Well, well,
here we are without a quorum and I thought I was going to
be late. (*To* MADDIE.) You'll know, of course, that a quorum
is a specified number of members of a committee whose
presence—God bless them—is necessary for the valid
transaction of business by that committee—got it? Good.
(CHAMBERLAIN *opens the* Daily Mirror *to the pin-up page.*
MCTEAZLE *helps* MADDIE *down the steps; her skirt comes away
in his hand.*)
Strewth!
(*After the freeze* MCTEAZLE *tries to shove the skirt at* MADDIE
who has sat down primly behind her desk, but COCKLEBURY-
SMYTHE *enters so* MCTEAZLE *sits on the skirt.*)

COCKLEBURY-SMYTHE: Do we have a quorum?

CHAMBERLAIN: Hello, Cocklebury-Smythe.

COCKLEBURY-SMYTHE: So glad you could come, Chamberlain.
You know Miss Gotobed?

CHAMBERLAIN (*over-reacts*): No.

COCKLEBURY-SMYTHE: Mr. Chamberlain—Miss Gotobed.

CHAMBERLAIN: I meant I didn't *know* her.

COCKLEBURY-SMYTHE: Of course you don't know her. All we need
now is our Chairman. I wish he'd get his clogs on.
(*The door opens and* WITHENSHAW, *the Chairman, enters. He
is a Lancastrian. He also carries newspapers and a brief case.*)

WITHENSHAW: There's trouble in t'*Mail*.

COCKLEBURY-SMYTHE: Mill.

WITHENSHAW: *Mail*. (*He throws the papers and his brief case on to
the table.*)

COCKLEBURY-SMYTHE: Oh yes.

WITHENSHAW (*at* MADDIE): And who have we got here?

MADDIE: I'm the clerk. Miss Gotobed.

WITHENSHAW: And I'm Malcolm Withyou! (*He laughs
uproariously.*) Malcolm Withyou!—'ee you've got to be
quick—Malcolm Withenshaw, Chairman of Select
Committee on Promiscuity in High Places. Have you got an
order of business? (*He snatches Chamberlain's piece of paper
off her desk.*) 'Forget Golden Goose, Selfridges——'

27

(MADDIE *snatches the paper out of his hand and hands him in the same movement a sealed envelope from her bag.*)

MADDIE: This is for you.

WITHENSHAW (*generally*): Before I saw bloody paper I was going to congratulate you all on a clean bill of health. You can't have a committee washing dirty linen in the corridors of power unless every member is above suspicion. (*On which he produces from the envelope a large pair of Y-front pants which he immediately shoves back into the envelope.*) The wheres and Y-fronts, the whys and wherefores of this Committee are clear to you all. Our presence here today is testimony to the trust the House has in us as individuals and that includes you Maddiemoiselle. (*To* MADDIE.) Though you have been completely unaware of it your private life has been under intense scrutiny by top man in Security Service, a man so senior that I can't even tell you his name——

MADDIE: Fanshawe.

WITHENSHAW: Fanshawe—and you passed test. (*He has been looking around for a place to put his pants, and decides on* MADDIE's *desk drawer.*) Indeed the fact that you've jumped over heads of many senior clerks indicates that you passed with flying knickers. (*This slip of the tongue is because he has discovered the knickers in the drawer; he drops them back and slams the drawer.*) So it is all the more unfortunate to find stuff in the press like following: Thank you Cockie.

(COCKLEBURY-SMYTHE *reads from the* Daily Mail.)

COCKLEBURY-SMYTHE: 'On the day the Select Committee on Moral Standards in Public Life is due to reconvene I ask—was it wise for one of the members to be seen holding hands under the table with a staggeringly voluptuous, titian-haired green eyed beauty in a West End restaurant at the weekend? And if so, was it modest to choose the Coq d'Or?'

(*Meanwhile,* WITHENSHAW *has finished scribbling a note.*)

WITHENSHAW: Right. Bloody smart alec. Still, least said soonest mended. (*He tosses the note, which is on white paper the size of an old-fashioned £5 note, on to* MADDIE's *desk.*) Now then, I think you have received prior copies of my draft report,

28

and we'll go through it paragraph by paragraph in the usual way——

MCTEAZLE: Excuse me. Are we now in session?

WITHENSHAW: What's quorum Miss Gotobed?

MADDIE: Is it a specified number of——

CHAMBERLAIN (*hurriedly*): Four, Mr. Chairman.

WITHENSHAW: Then we'll kick off. Get your pencil out, lass.

MADDIE: Do I have to write down what you say?

WITHENSHAW: I can see you know your way around these committees, Miss Gotobed. You do speedwriting I suppose?

MADDIE: Yes, if I'm given enough time.

WITHENSHAW: That's all right. You just tell us if we're going too fast. Here's a copy of my draft report, and appendix A, B, C, and D . . . (*He is giving her these things out of his brief case, into which he puts the envelope containing his pants.*) . . . so it'll just be a matter of keeping a record of amendments, if any.

COCKLEBURY-SMYTHE: Excuse me, Withenshaw, but isn't it rather unusual to have a report by a Select Committee before the Committee has had the advantage of considering the evidence?

WITHENSHAW: Yes, it is unusual, Mr. Cocklebury-Smythe, but this is an unusual situation. As you know sexual immorality unites all parties. This Committee isn't here to play politics. You'll have your chance with amendments, for which you can have all the time in the world. In fact the P.M. insists on it—he doesn't want us to rush into print, he wants a thorough job which he can present to the House the day before the Queen's Silver Jubilee, along with trade figures.

MCTEAZLE: Isn't that going to cause rather a lot of flak in the 1922 Committee and the P.L.P.?

WITHENSHAW: Very likely, but by that time, I'm happy to say, I'm going to be well out of it in the Lords—life peerage for services to arts.

COCKLEBURY-SMYTHE: Services to the *arts*?

WITHENSHAW: I'll have you bloody know Mrs. Withenshaw and I have personally donated the Botticelli-style painted ceiling in the Free Church Assembly Hall. I've bought and paid for more naked bums than you've had hot dinners.

COCKLEBURY-SMYTHE: I'm glad to say I've had more hot dinners.

WITHENSHAW: I speak sub-cathedra of course—no one else knows except Mrs. Withenshaw, and I shouldn't have told her—she's taken to wearing white gloves up to elbows to greyhounds. Anyway, what the P.M. wants is a unanimous report, if possible declaring—(*as if remembering*)—that there is no evidence that Members have engaged in scandalous conduct above the national average, or alternatively that they may have done in isolated cases, but are we going to judge grown responsible men in this day and age by the standards of Mrs. Grundy—whoever she may be—is it that old bag from Chorleywood South?

COCKLEBURY-SMYTHE: But what's the report based on if we aren't going to call any witnesses?

WITHENSHAW: What witnesses do you want to call?

COCKLEBURY-SMYTHE: Well . . . I personally wouldn't wish to call any——

MCTEAZLE: Hear, hear!

CHAMBERLAIN: Absolutely!

COCKLEBURY-SMYTHE: I've no time for stool pigeons admittedly——

MCTEAZLE: Hear, hear!

CHAMBERLAIN: Absolutely!

WITHENSHAW: There aren't any bloody witnesses. No one has seen anything. It's all bloody innuendo to sell newspapers in slack period.

ALL: Hear, hear!

WITHENSHAW: What with all the giant killers knocked out of Cup, and Ceylon versus Bangladesh—I don't call *that* a bloody test match—the papers naturally resort to sticking their noses into upper reaches of top drawers looking for hankie panties, etcetera. . . .

ALL: Hear, hear!

WITHENSHAW: I tell you, if those bloody pandas had got stuck in and produced a cuddly black and white nipper for London Zoo, it wouldn't be *us* in spotlight——

ALL: Hear, hear!

WITHENSHAW: Or Mark and Anne for that matter.

COCKLEBURY-SMYTHE: Steady on, Malcolm.

WITHENSHAW: I don't mean it would be black and white.

COCKLEBURY-SMYTHE: Can we move on?

WITHENSHAW: I was just making the point that there's nothing
to witness just because a member of this Committee is so
bowed down with the burden of representing his constituency, while trying to make a decent living in his spare
time, that he has to take his—homework—to lunch in a
West End restaurant.

ALL: Hear, hear!

CHAMBERLAIN: *Or* to dinner—pilloried for a beef stew in a
modest eating house with a professional appointment, for
all anyone knows a vicar's daughter worried sick about the
new motorway.

MCTEAZLE: Any cynic can make it look like a hole-in-the-corner
affair in an out-of-the-way nook like the Coq d'Or quite
probably is, many of these French places are——

COCKLEBURY-SMYTHE: Nor was it a case of holding hands under
the table.

ALL: Hear, hear!

COCKLEBURY-SMYTHE: Probably she was passing him the money
under the table, or vice versa.

MCTEAZLE: The table under the money——

COCKLEBURY-SMYTHE: —him passing *her* the money under the
table—probably a financially embarrassed lobbyist for
sexual equality taking an M.P. to a working dinner.

MCTEAZLE: Women's lib——

WITHENSHAW: One of those American bits.

COCKLEBURY-SMYTHE: Quite possibly——

WITHENSHAW: These Americans, they get in everywhere.

COCKLEBURY-SMYTHE: Far too many of them about.

MCTEAZLE: Hear, hear!

CHAMBERLAIN: Absolutely!

WITHENSHAW (*to* MADDIE): Would you care to take my appendix
out and pass it round—I've something of a reputation for
dry humour, you know. Yes, I once took a train journey
right across America . . .

(*He pauses at the sight of* MADDIE *in her slip.* MADDIE *has*

31

*picked up the sets of appendices and come out from behind her
desk and taken two steps before remembering her state of
undress, she pauses at the same moment, and then decides to
continue. Big Ben starts chiming the three-quarter hour.*
MADDIE *goes round the table placing documents in front of the
first couple of places. Big Ben finishes chiming the three-
quarter hour.*)
. . . but that's another story.
(*The door opens to admit* MRS. EBURY. *All look at her as she
speaks except* MCTEAZLE *who tries to hand* MADDIE *her skirt
unnoticed.* MADDIE *misses this, as she is intent on passing out
the rest of the appendices.*)

MRS. EBURY: I'm sorry to be late, Malcolm.

WITHENSHAW: Come right in, Deborah—we're just casting our
eye over the media. You're next to me, lass.
(MRS. EBURY *hangs up her coat. She also is carrying newspapers
and case. To get round the table she has to pass behind the
blackboard, as does* MADDIE *who is making slightly heavy
weather of sorting out appendices A, B, C, and D for each
member.* MRS. EBURY *and* MADDIE *cross over behind the
blackboard but do not emerge immediately. Meanwhile the*
CHAIRMAN *has opened the leader page of* The Times *and has
started reading aloud.*)

WITHENSHAW: '*Cherchez La Femme Fatale*. It needs no Gibbon
come from the grave to spell out the danger to good
government of a moral vacuum at the centre of power.
Even so, Rome did not fall in a day, and *mutatis mutandis* it
is not yet a case of *sauve qui peut* for the government——'
—what is all this?—'Admittedly the silence hangs heavy in
the House, no doubt on the principle of *qui s'excuse s'accuse,*
but we expect the electorate to take in its stride *cum grano
salis* stories that upwards of a hundred M.P.s are *in
flagrante delicto*, still more that the *demi-mondaine* in most
cases is a single and presumably exhausted Dubarry *de nos
jours*——' bloody 'ell.
(*To* MCTEAZLE *who has picked up the* Guardian.)
What does yours say?

MADDIE (*only her legs visible behind the blackboard*): Forget the

32

Golden Carriage, the Cooking Pot and the Coq d'Or.
Forget the Golden Carriage, the Watched Pot and the Coq
d'Or. Forget the Golden Pot, Claridges and the Watched
Cook . . .

(MADDIE's *speech is loud until* MCTEAZLE *interrupts with the*
Guardian, *but continues softly until* MCTEAZLE *reaches 'tedious,
or at any rate tendentious . . .' where it stops, to be heard
again on* MCTEAZLE's *'Quis custodiet . . .' and finally stopping
on* WITHENSHAW's *'Information'.)*

MCTEAZLE (*reading from the* Guardian): 'Spécialités de la Maison.
The House of Commons is no stranger to scandal or to
farce but it usually manages to arrange its follies so as to
keep the two separate. It would be tedious, or at any rate
tendentious, to give a *catalogue raisonné* of the, at a
Conservative estimate 63 Members of Parliament, and at a
Labour estimate 114, of whom the *homme moyen sensuel* on
the Clapham omnibus might well be asking, "Quis custodiet
ipsos custodes?" '

(MRS. EBURY *emerges during this final Latin phrase. Her hair,
which had been done up in a bun, is now about her shoulders
and her buttoned-up suit is in discreet disarray. She takes her
seat.*)

(*Continuing.*) '—and yet our information——'

(MADDIE *emerges from behind the blackboard.*)

WITHENSHAW (*scornfully*): Information! What does the editor of
Manchester Guardian know about anything—bloody young
pup—what's his name——

MADDIE (*putting documents in front of him*): Peter.

WITHENSHAW (*to* MRS. EBURY): Ah—I don't think you know Miss
Gotobed.

MRS. EBURY: How do you do?

(CHAMBERLAIN *picks up the* Daily Mirror.)

CHAMBERLAIN: 'How many cocks on the dung heap? We say too
many—see page 2.' (*He turns the page.*)

(MCTEAZLE *is surreptitiously trying to shove* MADDIE's *skirt at
her as she goes by. She doesn't notice, and he grabs at her
slip.*)

Strewth!

(ALL *but* MCTEAZLE *look at him*—ALL *freeze. Simultaneously* MADDIE'*s slip has come away in* MCTEAZLE'*s hand, leaving her wearing a revealing blouse, knickers, suspender belt, stockings and shoes.*

After the freeze MADDIE *sits down behind her desk.*

MCTEAZLE *now sits on the skirt and the slip.*)

(*To* MADDIE): Well, are you ready for it Miss Gotobed?

MADDIE: Yes.

WITHENSHAW: Well we seem to be a full complement except for Mr. French. Has anybody heard whether he's coming?

MRS. EBURY: I hope to God not.

WITHENSHAW: Mr. French always has the best interests of the House at heart. That is why he comes over as a sancti-monious busybody with an Energen roll where his balls ought to be—no need to start writing yet, Miss Gotobed.

MCTEAZLE: I don't know what the P.M. was thinking of.

COCKLEBURY-SMYTHE: I expect he was thinking of having a balanced committee to lend the kind of credibility to our report which has eluded him in public life.

WITHENSHAW (*to* MADDIE): Not yet. (*Stands.*) Now, as this Select Committee has, as it were, lost its Chairman of the last session, our first duty as a Committee is to make good that loss.

(*Very rapidly now.*)

COCKLEBURY-SMYTHE: Propose Mr. Withenshaw.

MCTEAZLE: Second.

WITHENSHAW: Any other nominations?

The question is put——

ALL: Aye.

WITHENSHAW: Thank you Mrs. Ebury and gentlemen. (*Sits.*) Let's get started. (*To* MADDIE.) Mr. Withenshaw called to chair. The Chairman's draft report, having been read for the first time—any objections to that?—thank you—was further considered as follows:

Paragraph 1. In performing the duty entrusted to them your Committee took as their guiding principle that it is the just and proper expectation of the electorate and the country at large, that its representatives in Parliament should bring

34

probity, honourable intent and decent conduct, not merely
to the discharge of the business of government but also to
their personal and social behaviour, which needs must stand
in an exemplary relationship to the behaviour of the British
people generally.

COCKLEBURY-SMYTHE: I must say that strikes an authentic
Lancastrian note. Who wrote this?

WITHENSHAW: Would you mind?

COCKLEBURY-SMYTHE: Was it the P.M.?

WITHENSHAW: No.

COCKLEBURY-SMYTHE: I'll know if it becomes Tennysonian, you
know.

WITHENSHAW: You're out of order, Mr. Cocklebury-Smythe.
(MADDIE *has her hand up, the other hand writing busily but
laboriously.*)
Not that bit, Miss Gotobed.

MADDIE: '. . . called to chair.'

COCKLEBURY-SMYTHE: *The* chair.

WITHENSHAW (*at* MADDIE'*s speed which is about 30 words a
minute*): '*The* chair. The Chair-man's draft report having
been read for the first time was further con-sider-ed as
fol-lows——' The next bit is the draft report which you've
got so you don't have to write it down again.

MADDIE (*with the document*): All this about setting an example?

WITHENSHAW: Yes.

MADDIE: You should tell them to mind their own business.

WITHENSHAW: Who?

MADDIE: Whoever it is who wants to know. It's a load of rubbish.

WITHENSHAW: What is?

MADDIE: People don't care what M.P.s do in their spare time,
they just want them to do their jobs properly bringing
down prices and everything.

WITHENSHAW: Yes, well . . .

MADDIE: Why don't they have a Select Committee to report on
what M.P.s have been up to in their *working* hours—that's
what people want to know.

COCKLEBURY-SMYTHE: It's rather more complicated than that—
er—Arab oil and . . .

35

(The following speeches overlap each other until the CHAIRMAN *calls the meeting to order.)*

CHAMBERLAIN: . . . the Unions.

COCKLEBURY-SMYTHE: M.P.s don't have the power they used to have, you know.

MCTEAZLE: Foreign exchange—the Bank of England.

MRS. EBURY: The multi-national companies.

MCTEAZLE: Not to mention government by Cabinet.

CHAMBERLAIN: Government by Cabal.

MRS. EBURY: Brussels.

COCKLEBURY-SMYTHE: The Whips.

WITHENSHAW: Just a minute—that'll do—come to order.

MADDIE: I'm sorry.

WITHENSHAW: Paragraph 2. Your Committee took it as self-evident that the consent to govern may be withheld if the people lose respect for the Commons either severally or as an institution, either through executive or constitutional deficiency, either on practical or moral grounds. It is on this latter ground—the morality of the honourable 600—that your Committee has fixed its lance, determined to ride fearlessly into the jaws of controversy.

COCKLEBURY-SMYTHE: It is the P.M., isn't it?

WITHENSHAW: I'm not saying it is, and anyway what's wrong with Her Majesty's first minister keeping a close watch on the interests of the people re clean living on the back benches.

MADDIE: It isn't the people, it's the newspapers.

MCTEAZLE: That's true.

COCKLEBURY-SMYTHE: Well the newspapers *are* the people in a sense—they are the channel of the government's answerability to the governed. The Fourth Estate of the realm speaking for the hearts and minds of the people.

MRS. EBURY: And on top of that they're as smug a collection of inaccurate, hypocritical, self-important, bullying, shoddily printed sick-bags as you'd hope to find in a month of Sundays, and dailies, and the weeklies aren't much better.

COCKLEBURY-SMYTHE: They're not all that inaccurate.

CHAMBERLAIN: You can't ignore them.

36

MADDIE: Nothing would happen if you did. They've got more people writing about football than writing about you and that's in the *cricket* season—they know what they're about.

COCKLEBURY-SMYTHE: The press, you see, is not just an ordinary commercial enterprise like selling haberdashery.

MADDIE: Yes it is.

COCKLEBURY-SMYTHE: Yes I know it is, but it is also the watchdog of democracy, which haberdashery, by and large, is not.

MADDIE: If the press is all that, you should be asking *them* about chasing after anything in a skirt, which they do. You should have a Select Committee on it—'Your Committee doesn't think it right for journalists to carry on as if there was no tomorrow.'

WITHENSHAW: Thank you——

MADDIE: You're just as entitled to enjoy yourself as they are.

WITHENSHAW: Thank you very much——

MADDIE: You should tell them to mind their own business.

WITHENSHAW: Paragraphs 1 and 2 read and agreed to.

MADDIE: *I* would——

(*The* CHAIRMAN *looks at her.*)

Sorry. (*She starts writing.*)

WITHENSHAW: Paragraph 3.

MADDIE (*with her hand up*): Paragraphs 1 and 2 . . .

WITHENSHAW: . . . read and agreed to. Paragraph 3.

MADDIE (*with her hand up*): . . . read and . . .

WITHENSHAW: . . . agreed to . . .

MADDIE: . . . agreed to . . .

WITHENSHAW: Paragraph 3.

MADDIE: Thank you. Sorry.

WITHENSHAW (*clears throat*): Your Committee and their predecessors in the last session have had before them the papers laid before the House including the written depositions (appendix A) and memoranda (appendix B).

(ALL *turn over to next page.*)

Paragraph 4. Your Committee also had before them a large assortment of press cuttings on this and related matters (appendix C). Your Committee did not feel that any purpose would be served by calling all the authors of these articles, which were in any case frequently anonymous or pseudonymous, and invariably uncorroborated.

MRS. EBURY: Amendment, Mr. Chairman.

WITHENSHAW: Yes, Mrs. Ebury.

MRS. EBURY: Paragraph 4, line 4. After 'invariably uncorroborated' insert 'and actuated by malice'.

WITHENSHAW: Amendment proposed. After 'invariably uncorroborated' insert 'and actuated by malice'. In favour?

ALL (*except* COCKLEBURY-SMYTHE): Aye.

WITHENSHAW: Against.

COCKLEBURY-SMYTHE: No.

WITHENSHAW: Amendment stands. (*To* MADDIE.) All right?

MADDIE: Act . . .

MCTEAZLE: . . . u . . . a . . . (*pause*) . . . ted

CHAMBERLAIN: by . . .

MADDIE: by . . .

COCKLEBURY-SMYTHE: Malice.

MADDIE: Mal . . .

MRS. EBURY: iss . . . (MADDIE *looks up*) . . . ice.

WITHENSHAW: Mrs. Ebury in brackets.

MADDIE (*pause*): In brack-ets.

WITHENSHAW: No, no just put her in brackets. (*Apologetically.*) It's her first time you know.

ALL: Oh yes . . . naturally . . . time to settle down . . .

WITHENSHAW: Very good. Paragraph now ends 'invariably uncorroborated and actuated by malice'.

CHAMBERLAIN: Amendment, Mr. Chairman.

WITHENSHAW: Yes, Mr. Chamberlain.

CHAMBERLAIN: Insert after 'malice' the words 'and cynical pursuit of cheap sensationalism'.

WITHENSHAW: Amendment put. In favour?

ALL (*except* COCKLEBURY-SMYTHE): Aye.

WITHENSHAW: Against?

COCKLEBURY-SMYTHE: No.

WITHENSHAW: Amendment stands.

CHAMBERLAIN (*to* MADDIE): Me in brackets.

MADDIE: . . . cyn . . .

CHAMBERLAIN (*at* MADDIE's *speed*): . . . ical pursuit

MADDIE: . . . ical purs . . .

CHAMBERLAIN: . . . uit of . . .

MADDIE: . . . suit of . . .

CHAMBERLAIN: . . . cheap sens . . .

MADDIE: . . . cheap sense . . .

CHAMBERLAIN: . . . ationalism.

> (*This may have been fractionally faster than the last amendment.*)

MADDIE: . . . ationalism.

WITHENSHAW: That's it. You see you're improving all the time.

ALL: Oh yes . . . getting the hang of it . . .

MCTEAZLE: Amendment, Mr. Chairman. (*He scribbles on a piece of paper.*)

WITHENSHAW: Yes, Mr. McTeazle.

MCTEAZLE: After 'sensationalism' insert 'through a degrading obsession with dirty linen among the Pecksniffs of Fleet Street'. (*He hands paper to* MADDIE.)

WITHENSHAW: I don't think these unnatural practices are very . . .

MCTEAZLE: He's a character in *Dombey and Son*——

WITHENSHAW (*lying*): I am well aware he's a character in *Dombey and Son*.

COCKLEBURY-SMYTHE: Chuzzlewit.

WITHENSHAW (*with spirit*): Chuzzlewit yourself, Cockie. Amendment put. Favour?

ALL (*except* COCKLEBURY-SMYTHE): Aye.

WITHENSHAW: Against.

COCKLEBURY-SMYTHE: No.

WITHENSHAW: Amendment stands. Paragraph now reads——

COCKLEBURY-SMYTHE: Amendment, Mr. Chairman.

WITHENSHAW: Yes, Mr. Cocklebury-Smythe.

COCKLEBURY-SMYTHE: Before the words 'and a cynical pursuit etcetera' insert the words 'in some cases, possibly'.

WITHENSHAW: Amendment put. All in fa . . .r?

COCKLEBURY-SMYTHE: Aye.

WITHENSHAW: Against?

ALL (*except* COCKLEBURY-SMYTHE): No.

WITHENSHAW: Amendment fails. (*To* MADDIE.) Paragraph now reads . . .

MADDIE (*reading from the draft*): 'Paragraph 4. Your Committee also had before them a large assortment of press cuttings on this and related matters (appendix C). Your Committee did not feel that any purpose would be served by calling all the authors of these articles, which were in any case frequently anonymous or pseudonymous, and invariably uncorroborated (*reads from her notebook*) and actuated by malice and a cynical pursuit of cheap sensationalism (*reads from paper passed to her by* MCTEAZLE) through a degrading obsession with dirty linen among the Pecksniffs of Fleet Street. I'm sitting on your slip. (*To* MCTEAZLE.) Sorry.

MCTEAZLE (*looking at the others*): A slip—just a slip.

WITHENSHAW: The question is put that the paragraph stand as part of the report.

COCKLEBURY-SMYTHE: Division, Mr. Chairman.

WITHENSHAW: Division, Committee divided.

Mr. Chamberlain.

CHAMBERLAIN: Aye.

(MADDIE'*s hand has gone up.*)

WITHENSHAW (*to* MADDIE): The Com-mit-tee div-id-ed.

MADDIE: . . . divided. Then what do I do?

WITHENSHAW: Then you draw a line down the middle. (*The* CHAIRMAN *goes to the blackboard and draws a line down the middle and generally demonstrates on the blackboard. But he spells 'noes' as 'Nose'.*) You write 'ayes' up there on the left and 'noes' up there on the other side and when I call out their names you write them down on one side or the other, according to what they say.

Mr. Chamberlain.

CHAMBERLAIN: Aye.

WITHENSHAW: Mrs. Ebury.

MRS. EBURY: Aye.

WITHENSHAW: Mr. McTeazle.

MCTEAZLE: Aye.

WITHENSHAW: Mr. Cocklebury-Smythe—National Union of Journalists.

COCKLEBURY-SMYTHE: No—I have to make a living in my spare time too, you know.

WITHENSHAW: Three—one.

MADDIE: Just like the football results.

WITHENSHAW (*warmly*): Just like the football results. Isn't it?

ALL: Oh yes . . . so it is . . . what a good thought. . . .

WITHENSHAW: Paragraph 4, read and agreed to. Mr. Cocklebury-Smythe, M.P., N.U.J.; dissenting.

Paragraph 5.

MADDIE: You don't need all these paragraphs, you know . . .

WITHENSHAW: 'Your Committee . . .'

MADDIE: You're just playing into their hands.

(WITHENSHAW *glares at her.*)

It's just my opinion.

WITHENSHAW: Paragraph 5. 'Your Committee . . .'

MCTEAZLE (*to* MADDIE): Whose hands?

WITHENSHAW (*to* MCTEAZLE): For God's sake——

MADDIE: The press. The more you accuse them of malice and inaccuracy, the more you're admitting that they've got a right to poke their noses into your private life. All this fuss! The whole report can go straight in the waste-paper basket. All you need is one paragraph saying that M.P.s have got just as much right to enjoy themselves in their own way as anyone else, and Fleet Street can take a running jump.

WITHENSHAW: Miss Gotobed, you may not be aware that the clerk traditionally refrains from drafting the report of a Select Committee.

MADDIE: And anyway, there's no malice in it. You've got that wrong, too.

WITHENSHAW: Paragraph 5!

COCKLEBURY-SMYTHE: She's quite right, of course. It's simplistic to speak of malice.

WITHENSHAW: Smart alec-paragraphs about innocent tripe-and-onions with titian voluptuaries?—if that's not malice I don't know what is.

MADDIE: They only write it up because of each other writing it up. Then they try to write it up *more* than each other—it's like a competition, you see.

COCKLEBURY-SMYTHE (*puzzled*): A free press is competitive naturally . . .

MADDIE: No, the *writers*. They're not writing it for the people, they're writing it for the writers writing it on the other papers. 'Look what I've got that you haven't got.' There don't have to be any *people* reading it at all so long as there's a few journalists around to say, 'Old Bill got a good one there!' That's what they're doing it for. I thought you'd have worked that out by now.

COCKLEBURY-SMYTHE (*taken aback*): Not really.

MADDIE: You see, you don't know the first thing about journalism.

(ALL *laugh at* COCKLEBURY-SMYTHE. MADDIE *stands up— unfolds one of the newspapers on her desk and holds it in front of her, between her and the Committee so that it obscures her skirtless, slipless state of undress from the Committee but not from the audience. She walks to the front of the committee table. The Committee react to the photograph on the paper facing them.*)

The *pictures* are for the people.

ALL: Strewth!

(*The door opens to admit* MR. FRENCH, *who enters and hangs up his coat. As the Committee look at him,* MADDIE *turns and returns to her desk, folding the newspaper.*)

CHAMBERLAIN: Hello, French.

FRENCH (*to* CHAIRMAN, *without seeing* MADDIE): Mea maxima culpa.

COCKLEBURY-SMYTHE: Merde.

WITHENSHAW: All present and correct. (*To* MADDIE.) Amend list of members present.

COCKLEBURY-SMYTHE (*to* MADDIE): French . . .

MADDIE (*to* FRENCH): Enchantée . . .

COCKLEBURY-SMYTHE: No . . . no . . . Mr. French, Miss Gotobed.

FRENCH: How do you do, so sorry to interrupt. (*Looking at the blackboard.*) What's that? (*He sits down. He has a white silk handkerchief showing in his breast pocket and he uses this to wipe his brow. He does this once or twice during the scene.*)

WITHENSHAW: A blackboard. No . . . No . . . I was just . . .

(He looks round for something to wipe the board but there's nothing to hand so he takes the underpants out of the brief case and uses them.) . . . our clerk, Miss Gotobed, has been assigned to this Committee on the recommendation of I think you-know-who——

FRENCH: Who?

MADDIE: Fanshawe.

WITHENSHAW: —need I say more? Her experience of committee work is not extensive and I was just explaining one or two of the finer points.

FRENCH: Of course.

WITHENSHAW: Well, as I was saying on that last Division Cocklebury-Smythe is under the 'noes'.

MCTEAZLE: Pecksniff. Chuzzlewit.

COCKLEBURY-SMYTHE: Yes——

MCTEAZLE: Sorry.

COCKLEBURY-SMYTHE: Not at all.

(The CHAIRMAN *has hurriedly wiped the board clean and is putting his underpants back into his brief case.)*

FRENCH: What is *that*?

WITHENSHAW: Pair of briefs.

FRENCH: What are they doing in there?

WITHENSHAW: It's a brief case. Paragraph 5.

FRENCH: What stage are we at, Mr. Chairman?

WITHENSHAW: Second reading of the draft report, Mr. French.

FRENCH: When was the first reading?

WITHENSHAW: Haven't you gone through it?

FRENCH: Yes. Last night.

WITHENSHAW: That's when it was. Do you really want me to go through the whole thing again? It's pure formality.

FRENCH: That may be so, but there is a way of doing things, and if we're not going to do them in that way let it be shown in the proceedings of this Select Committee that the Committee voted on that point.

WITHENSHAW: Very well.

(Very rapidly.)

COCKLEBURY-SMYTHE: Propose.

MCTEAZLE: Second.

WITHENSHAW: Favour.

ALL (*except* FRENCH): Aye.

WITHENSHAW: Against.

FRENCH: No.

WITHENSHAW: Carried.

(*Even more rapidly, absolute breakneck speed because it's pure ritual.*)

FRENCH: Division.

WITHENSHAW: Division. Mr. Chamberlain.

CHAMBERLAIN: Aye.

WITHENSHAW: Mr. Cocklebury-Smythe.

COCKLEBURY-SMYTHE: Aye.

WITHENSHAW: Mrs. Ebury.

MRS. EBURY: Aye.

WITHENSHAW: Mr. French.

FRENCH: No.

WITHENSHAW: Mr. McTeazle.

MCTEAZLE: Aye.

WITHENSHAW: Carried.

MADDIE: Line down the middle?

WITHENSHAW: Line down the middle.

(FRENCH *is slightly surprised by this.*)

Committee divided 4–1.

MADDIE: Home win.

WITHENSHAW: Home win. Mr. French lone scorer for visitors.

FRENCH: I beg your pardon?

WITHENSHAW: The terminology of committee practice is in a constant state of organic change, Mr. French. If you can't keep up you'll be no use to us. Paragraph 5.

FRENCH: Excuse me, Mr. Chairman.

WITHENSHAW: Yes, Mr. French?

FRENCH: We haven't heard any evidence.

WITHENSHAW: Evidence about what, Mr. French?

FRENCH: You know very well, evidence about what—evidence about 128 Members of Parliament making fools of themselves over a latter day Dubarry and bringing the House into public ridicule and disrepute.

WITHENSHAW (*heatedly*): Do you believe everything you read in

44

the papers, Mr. French?

FRENCH (*also heatedly*): I wish to have this exchange of views recorded in the minutes.

WITHENSHAW (*at* MADDIE'*s speed, to* FRENCH): Do you believe everything you read in the papers, Mr. French?

COCKLEBURY-SMYTHE (*at* MADDIE'*s speed, to* FRENCH): It is true that some of us have been feeling up . . .

(*Pause.* ALL *react to 'feeling up' with some trepidation.* COCKLEBURY-SMYTHE *continues innocently.*)

. . . to now that evidence as such does not exist in these matters.

ALL: Hear (*pause*) hear!

(FRENCH *has taken some time to cotton on to the reason for the rate of speech, because the other Members have tactfully ignored* MADDIE. FRENCH *goes through various stages of bewilderment and suspicion before noting* MADDIE'*s writing speed.*)

FRENCH: Just a minute—excuse me—is Miss Gotobed a secretary/clerk of the Clerks Department?

WITHENSHAW: Why d'you ask?

COCKLEBURY-SMYTHE: She can do forty words a minute.

FRENCH: Shorthand?

COCKLEBURY-SMYTHE: No—talking.

MRS. EBURY: She is seconded from the Home Office.

FRENCH: What is her job there? A manicurist?

MADDIE: I'm a typist.

WITHENSHAW: Miss Gotobed has been recommended, by different people, I understand, in a period of some difficulty.

FRENCH: I was expecting to have Mr. Barraclough, a man of irreproachable credentials——

WITHENSHAW: I believe he has taken early retirement for personal reasons.

MADDIE: Barry has?

WITHENSHAW: I must insist that we get on with the proper business of this Committee.

(FRENCH *getting hysterical.*)

FRENCH: The proper business of this Committee is to examine witnesses!

45

WITHENSHAW: If you will be so patient, Mr. French, you will be reminded that paragraph 5 will take cognizance of the evidence heard by this Select Committee in its previous incarnation during last session.

FRENCH: I was not a member then.

WITHENSHAW: None of us were members then, Mr. French. This Committee has suffered the resignation for personal reasons of the previous membership—and for medical reasons, of the previous chairman, Sir Joshua Matlock who dislocated his hip——

MADDIE: Both hips——

WITHENSHAW: Both hips. Nevertheless that evidence, such as it was, is something which I have given due consideration in preparing this draft report. (*To* MADDIE.) Now. (*Generally, at* MADDIE's *speed.*) Paragraph 5 read as follows. (*Normal speed.*)

(ALL *turn to proper place in draft report.*)

Your Committee also had the advantage of having a number of distinguished journalists regaling the Committee with the moving and heroic tale of the struggle of the British press from time immemorial to become independent watchdogs of the people's right to know; with many reference to flames, torches, swords, pens, grails and the general impedimenta of chivalrous quest . . .

COCKLEBURY-SMYTHE (*giggles*): Tennyson's Disease.

WITHENSHAW: . . . Unfortunately, the witnesses were considerably less helpful on the subject of their sources for the unsubstantiated speculations which were the chief and only reason for the witnesses being called. In the words of Alfred Lord . . . (*pause*) your Committee therefore was unable to conclude that the aforesaid speculations had any basis in fact——

MCTEAZLE: Amendment, Mr. Chairman.

WITHENSHAW: Yes, Mr. McTeazle.

MCTEAZLE: Paragraph 5 line 1 before the word 'journalists' to omit the word 'distinguished'.

FRENCH: Then we should examine the editors.

WITHENSHAW: Can we dispose of this amendment?

FRENCH: What about the leading article in this week's *New Statesman*? It refers to private information.

WITHENSHAW (*jeers*): Private information? Gossiping over Bristol Cream in Vincent Square?

FRENCH: That is your assumption only.

WITHENSHAW: Where else would he pick anything up—young pup—what's-his-name——

MADDIE: Tony.

FRENCH: The editors must be in possession of hard information otherwise they would not let the reporters publish the rumours.

WITHENSHAW: Don't be a fool, man.

COCKLEBURY-SMYTHE: I'm afraid that that does not always follow, Mr. French.

FRENCH: What about *The Times*? You're not suggesting that the editor of *The Times*—a man of irreproachable credentials—— (*Heatedly to* MADDIE.) Mr. French proposed: that the editor of *The Times* . . .

WITHENSHAW: Not so quickly please.

FRENCH (*slowly*): Mr. French proposed . . .

MCTEAZLE (*to* MRS. EBURY): What do you think of it so far?

MRS. EBURY: Rubbish!

FRENCH (*continues slowly*): . . . that the editor of *The Times* (*resuming his normal speed*)—whatever his name is——

MADDIE: Willy.

WITHENSHAW (*impatiently*): This is already dealt with in appendix B. *The Times* has published no rumours, it's only reported facts, namely that less responsible papers are publishing certain rumours. *That* is a written deposition from the editor (*rifling through appendix B*).

FRENCH: It is not. It is a memorandum from one of the Whips who bumped into him in the interval at Covent Garden. Can any one of us truthfully say that we have *really* examined the editor of *The Times*?

CHAMBERLAIN: No.

COCKLEBURY-SMYTHE: No.

WITHENSHAW: No.

MRS. EBURY: No.

MCTEAZLE: No.

MADDIE: Not really.

(*Or from Stage Right round the table.*)

WITHENSHAW: I must insist that we get back to bloody amendment. The question is put—to omit in line one of paragraph 5 the word 'distinguished' before the word 'journalists'. All in favour.

ALL (*except* COCKLEBURY-SMYTHE *and* FRENCH): Aye.

WITHENSHAW: Against.

COCKLEBURY-SMYTHE: ⎱ No.
FRENCH: ⎰

WITHENSHAW: Arsenal 3 Newcastle 2. Scorers McTeazle, Chamberlain and Ebury for Arsenal. French and Cocklebury-Smythe, own goal, for Newcastle.

FRENCH: What the hell are you talking about?

WITHENSHAW: Kindly watch your language—you're not on terraces now, y'know.

MRS. EBURY: And there are ladies present.

FRENCH: All right! Cards on the table! I didn't want to be the one to bring this up, but I rather expected to learn on arriving here today that one of our number—I exclude Mrs. Ebury of course—had seen fit to resign from this Committee. I refer to the paragraph in today's *Mail* about the tête-à-tête at the Côte d'Or.

MRS. EBURY: Cock.

FRENCH: Coq d'Or.

MRS. EBURY: Double cock.

FRENCH: Without either a resignation or alternatively our joint repudiation of the story I don't see how this Committee can have the confidence of the House.

MRS. EBURY: Ballocks.

FRENCH: That is not an expression which I would have associated with you, Mrs. Ebury.

MRS. EBURY: I don't need you to tell me my problems.

WITHENSHAW (*aside to* MADDIE): The Committee deliberated.

FRENCH: I find the Committee's silence on this point significant.

WITHENSHAW: Well, we all thought it was you.

FRENCH: I left for my constituency on Friday evening and

48

returned this morning. The only meal I've had this weekend in a London restaurant was tea on Friday at the Golden Egg in Victoria Street.

COCKLEBURY-SMYTHE: L'Oeuf d'Or?

MCTEAZLE: Were you with a woman?

FRENCH: I was with the Dean of St. Paul's.

MCTEAZLE: Is she titian-haired?

CHAMBERLAIN: Come off it McTeazle. (*Kindly to* FRENCH.) French, can anyone corroborate your story?

FRENCH: The Dean of St. Paul's can.

CHAMBERLAIN: Apart from her.

FRENCH: We had Jumbo Chickenburgers Maryland with pickled eggs and a banana milkshake. The waitress will remember me.

CHAMBERLAIN: Why?

FRENCH: I was sick on her shoes.

COCKLEBURY-SMYTHE: Your story smacks of desperation. Even so you have done us the honour of volunteering your account, so let me reciprocate. I was at various times at Crockford's, Claridges and the Golden Cock, Clock, the Old Clock in Golden Square, not the Coq d'Or.

CHAMBERLAIN: I was at the Crock of Gold, Selfridges and the Green Cockatoo.

MCTEAZLE: I was at the Cockatoo, too, and the Charing Cross, the Open Door, the Golden Ox and the Cuckoo Clock.

WITHENSHAW: I was at the Cross Cook, the Fighting Cocks, the Green Door, the Crooked Grin and the Golden Carriages. (*What is happening is difficult to explain but probably quite easy to recognize: the four of them have instinctively joined in an obscuration, each for his own defence. By the time the* CHAIRMAN *speaks they have all begun to send* FRENCH *up.*)

COCKLEBURY-SMYTHE: I forgot—I was at the Golden Carriages as well as Claridges, and the Odd Sock and the Cocked Hat.

WITHENSHAW: I didn't see you at the Cocked Hat—I went on to the Cox and Box.

MCTEAZLE: I was at the Cox and Box, and the Cooks Door, the Old Chest, the Dorchester, the Chesty Cook and—er—Luigi's.

49

ALL: Luigi's?

MCTEAZLE: At King's Cross.

CHAMBERLAIN: I was at King's Cross; in the Cross Keys and the Coal Hole, the Golden Goose, the Coloured Coat and the Côte d'Azur.

COCKLEBURY-SMYTHE: I was at the Côte d'Azur——

WITHENSHAW: So was I.

MRS. EBURY: I was at the Coq d'Or.

CHAMBERLAIN (*incautiously*): I was at the Coq d'Or too.

(*Short pause but everybody comes to his rescue.*)

MCTEAZLE: So was I.

COCKLEBURY-SMYTHE: The Coq d'Or, oh yes, I was at the Coq d'Or.

WITHENSHAW: I saw you there—I was there with a voluptuous young woman.

COCKLEBURY-SMYTHE: Good heavens, I hope you didn't see me with mine.

CHAMBERLAIN: Fantastic woman I took there—titian hair, green eyes, dress cut down to here.

MCTEAZLE: We held hands under the table—(*with a crude gesture*) voluptuous, you've no idea.

WITHENSHAW: Don't talk to me about voluptuous—mine was titian like two Botticellis fighting their way out of a hammock.

(*During the above speech* FRENCH *is becoming increasingly agitated, and* MADDIE *increasingly angry. She gets out her copy of the* Sun *and opens it to the centre page spread.*)

COCKLEBURY-SMYTHE: Wonderful figure of a woman——

FRENCH (*shouts*): One of you is telling the truth! Where's the *Mail*!

(MADDIE *gets up and crosses to* FRENCH, *holding the* Sun. MADDIE *slams the* Sun *down on the table in front of* FRENCH, *open at the centre page spread and stands back to await his reaction.*)

WITHENSHAW: That's the *Sun*.

(FRENCH *does an enormous double-take at the pin-up.*)

FRENCH (*shrieks*): Aagh!—it's you!!

MADDIE: Yes.

(FRENCH *grabs* MADDIE *by the back of the blouse as she moves to go back to her desk; buttons pop and fly leaving* FRENCH *holding her blouse and* MADDIE *in her bra.*)

ALL (*looking at* MADDIE): Strewth!

(MADDIE *walks to her seat, taps her pencil on the desk.*)

MADDIE (*reading*): Paragraph 6.

FRENCH: Maddie Takes It Down!

'Madeleine Gotobed, twenty-one, is a model secretary in Whitehall where she says her ambition is to be Permanent Under Secretary. Meanwhile, titian-haired, green-eyed Maddie loves being taken out, but says the men tend to look down on a figure like hers—whenever they get the chance!'—disgusting—'Matching bra and suspender belt, Fenwicks £5.35. French knickers, Janet Reger £8.95.' (*To* MADDIE.) You were in the Coq d'Or!

(*The Division Bell goes off.*)

MADDIE: I was in the Coq d'Or, the Golden Ox, Box Hill, Claridges and Crockford's——

WITHENSHAW: Division bell, Mr. French.

MADDIE: —and the Charing Cross, the Dorchester, the Green Cockatoo, Selfridges and the Salt Beef Bar in Rupert Street with Deborah and Douglas and Cockie and Jock.

(MADDIE *has pointed to these four. Pause—*WITHENSHAW *looks relieved.*)

And with Malcolm in the Metropole——

(*The Committee's next words are just rattled off underneath* MADDIE's *speech which continues without pause.*)

WITHENSHAW: Move to adjourn.

COCKLEBURY-SMYTHE: Second.

WITHENSHAW: All in favour.

ALL (*except* FRENCH): Aye.

WITHENSHAW: Meeting adjourned for ten minutes.

(*The Committee hurriedly shuffle a few pieces of paper together, leaving all the newspapers behind, and arrange themselves to make their exits in a body, ignoring* MADDIE, *who chants on.*)

MADDIE (*continuing until all but* FRENCH *have left*): . . . and in the Mandarin, the Mirabelle and the Star of Asia in the Goldhawk Road. I was with Freddie and Reggie and Algy

and Bongo and Arthur and Cyril and Tom and Ernest and
Bob and the other Bob and Pongo at the Ritz and the Red
Lion, the Lobster Pot and Simpson's in the Strand—I was
at the Poule au Pot and the Coq au Vin and the Côte
d'Azur and Foo Luk Fok and the Grosvenor House and
Luigi's and Lacy's and the Light of India with Johnny and
Jackie and Jerry and Joseph and Jimmy, and in the Berkeley,
Biancis, Blooms and Muldoons with Micky and Michael
and Mike and Michelle—I was in the Connaught with
William and in the Westbury with Corkie and in the
Churchill with Chalky. I was at the Duke of York, the Duke
of Clarence and the Old Duke and the King Charles and
the Three Kings and the Kings Arms and the Army and
Navy Salad Bar with Tony and Derek and Bertie and
Plantagenet and Bingo.

(*During the above speech the Committee all exit through the
wrong door, return and re-exit. The door closes, leaving only*
FRENCH *with* MADDIE.)

(*Yells after them.*) And I wouldn't have bothered if I'd
known it was supposed to be a secret—who needs it?
(*Normal voice.*) I sometimes wonder if it's worthwhile
trying to teach people, don't you Mr. French?

FRENCH: Miss Gotobed, this is going to teach them a lesson
they'll never forget.

MADDIE: I hope so.

FRENCH: I have to go and vote. Please be here in about ten
minutes. (*He approaches her with the blouse still in hand.*)

MADDIE: Excuse me . . . (*She takes the blouse.*) . . . Somebody's
˜coming.

(*At this moment a loud voice is heard approaching.*)
Could you show me the ladies cloakroom.
(*She grabs the rest of her clothes and her handbag.* FRENCH
*takes her coat from the rack and puts it over her shoulders and
opens the door.* MADDIE *exits,* FRENCH *follows. As soon as the
door closes, the other opens and two men enter—but they are
in another play.*)

NEW-FOUND-LAND

A play in one act

Characters

ARTHUR   A very junior Home Office Official
BERNARD   A very senior Home Office Official

The House of Commons overspill meeting room in the tower of Big Ben, set as for Dirty Linen. *A lot of newspapers and reports are lying around on the main committee table.*

(ARTHUR *appears carrying a file of papers and shouts loudly into the door through which he enters, as though calling to someone at a distance.*)

ARTHUR (*shouts*): Here's an empty one!

> (BERNARD *enters immediately.* ARTHUR *shouts at him at the same volume. Everything* ARTHUR *says has to be shouted, throughout.*)
> It's the only one. The Minister said up here—he'll find us all right.
> (*They approach the table and sit at it.*)

BERNARD: Frightful mess.

> (ARTHUR *shuffling newspapers comes across something.*)

ARTHUR: Strewth!!

> (*An appallingly loud noise as Big Ben strikes four from just over their heads.* ARTHUR *flinches.* BERNARD *looks around vaguely. The last stroke finally dies away.*)

BERNARD: What was that?

ARTHUR: Four o'clock.

> (*Considerable pause.* BERNARD *takes out his wallet and an envelope containing a very old £5 note.*)

BERNARD: I bet you have not seen one of these for a while. . . .
It's a fiver I once won off Lloyd George, you know.

ARTHUR: Yes.

BERNARD: It's a good story. . . .

ARTHUR: Very, very good.

BERNARD: I was a green young man at the time, and he was . . .

whatdoyoucallit . . . ?

ARTHUR: Prime Minister.

BERNARD: Prime Minister. Even so, I knew him quite well, or rather my father did.

ARTHUR: Your father knew Lloyd George, yes.

BERNARD: He'd come to our house in Queen Anne Place. You could hear Big Ben from there. That's what reminded me.

ARTHUR: Yes.

This is the file on that applicant for British citizenship. What do you think? (*He moves to sit next to* BERNARD *so that he can speak loudly into his ear. He has a bulky file, including a photograph, to show* BERNARD.)

BERNARD: What?

ARTHUR: These naturalization papers. We're supposed to be advising the Minister.

(BERNARD *examines the document at considerable length.*)

ARTHUR: I'd like to have your opinion.

(*Finally* BERNARD *raps the document authoritatively.*)

BERNARD: This is an application for British naturalization.

ARTHUR: Yes. Does he look all right to you?

BERNARD: He's got a beard. The Minister won't like that.

ARTHUR (*nods*): No, then.

(ARTHUR *closes the file decisively.*)

BERNARD: He asked me for my views about French, you know.

ARTHUR: French?

BERNARD: Poor French. Out of touch. Do you know what he said to me about French?

ARTHUR: Who—the Minister?

BERNARD: Know what he said?

ARTHUR: What?

BERNARD (*shouts*): Do you know what he said about French? (*Normal voice.*) Called him a booby.

ARTHUR (*gives up*): Really.

(*Considerable pause.*)

BERNARD: I was in Belgium, having a look round the village church of Etienne St.-Juste, when I had the good fortune to receive a slight injury. The morning after my return to London, I remember, was one of those rare February days when winter seems to make an envious and premature clutch at the spring to come. I breakfasted by the window. The panes of glass in the window suddenly pulsed (*makes the sound*)—woomph-woomph—as though alive to the shock-waves of distant guns. I started to sob. But it was only a motor coming up the road. It stopped. The doorbell jangled below stairs, and then there was a knock at the morning room. Lloyd George was shown in. My father had already left for the City, as he liked to put it. He owned an emporium of Persian and oriental carpets in Cheapside, which was indeed in the City, and that is where he had gone. So there I was, a young lieutenant, barely blooded, talking to the Prime Minister of the day, and receiving ribald compliments on the shell splinter lodged in my lower abdomen. The shell itself had made a rather greater impact on the church of Etienne St.-Juste. I explained my father's absence, but Lloyd George was in no hurry to leave. It was then that he made his remark about French. 'What do they say in the field?' he asked me. 'Were they glad to see him go?' I replied tactfully that we all felt every confidence in Field-Marshal Haig. 'Yes,' he said, 'Haig's the man to finish this war. French was a booby.' That is what he said. (*Pause.*) Presently, Big Ben was heard to strike ten o'clock. Lloyd George at once asked me whether it was possible to see Big Ben from the upstairs window. I said that it was not. 'Surely you're wrong,' he said, 'are you absolutely certain?' 'Absolutely certain, Prime Minister.' He replied that he found it difficult to believe and would like to see for himself. I assured him that there was no need. The fact was, my mother was upstairs in bed making out her dinner table: she had the understandable, though to me unwelcome, desire to show me off during my leave. Lloyd George pressed the point, and finally said, 'I will bet you £5 that I can see Big Ben from Marjorie's window.' 'Very well,' I said, and we went upstairs. I explained to my mother that the Prime Minister and I had a bet on. She received us gaily, just as though she were in her drawing room, Lloyd George went to the window and pointed.

'Bernard,' he said, 'I see from Big Ben that it is four minutes past the hour. The £5 which you have lost,' he continued, 'I will spend on vast quantities of flowers for your mother by way of excusing this intrusion. It is small price to pay,' he said, 'for the lesson that you must never pit any of the five Anglo-Saxon senses against the Celtic sixth sense.' 'Prime Minister,' I said, 'I'm afraid Welsh intuition is no match for English cunning. Big Ben is the name of the bell, not the clock.' He paid up at once . . .

. . . and that was a fiver which I can tell you I have never spent. (*He shows the note to* ARTHUR.)
How they laughed. 'Marjorie,' he said, 'that boy of yours does not miss a trick.' I left then, to take a cab to Dr. Slocombe in Pall Mall. When I returned I saw Lloyd George alone for the last time. He was coming down the steps. Nervousness caused me to commit the social solecism of trying to return him his money, 'Keep it,' he said, 'I never spent a better £5.' He got into the back of the motor and waved cheerily and called, 'You will go far in the Army.' Well, he was wrong about that. And he was not entirely right about Haig either. It was the Americans who saved *him*.

ARTHUR: This applicant is American.

(*Pause.*)

BERNARD: An *American* with a beard? Oh dear . . . of course, in those days it was the other way round. It was difficult to get British nationality *without* a beard. A well bearded and moustachioed man stood an excellent chance with the Home Secretary. A man with a moustache but no beard was often given the benefit of the doubt. A man with a beard and *no* moustache, on the other hand, was considered unreliable and probably fraudulent, and usually had to remain American for the rest of his life. Does he have property?

(*From here on* ARTHUR *refers to the file.*)

ARTHUR: He is associated with a stable in Kentish Town.

BERNARD: Epsom Downs?

ARTHUR: No—Kentish Town.

BERNARD: A racing stable?

ARTHUR: It seems to be more of a farm really. . . .
　　(*Considerable pause.*)
BERNARD: Did you say he farms in Kentish Town?
ARTHUR: Yes.
BERNARD: Arable or pasture?
ARTHUR: It does seem odd doesn't it?
BERNARD: I imagine that good farming land would be at a
　　premium in North London. Is he prosperous?
ARTHUR: He has an income of £10.50 per week.
BERNARD: Hardly a pillar of the community, even with free milk
　　and eggs.
ARTHUR: No.
BERNARD: He is either a very poor farmer indeed, or a farmer of
　　genius—depending on which part of Kentish Town he
　　farms.
ARTHUR: He's not exactly a farmer I don't think . . . he has
　　other interests. Publishing. And he runs some sort of bus
　　service.
BERNARD: Publishing and buses? And a farm. Bit of a gadfly is
　　he?
ARTHUR: Yes. And community work.
BERNARD: They all say that.
ARTHUR: Yes.
BERNARD: Anything else?
ARTHUR: There's a theatrical side to him.
BERNARD: Do you mean he waves his arms around?
ARTHUR: No—no—he writes plays, and puts them on and so on.
　　He seems to have some kind of theatre.
BERNARD: Oh dear, yes. A theatrical farmer with buses on the
　　side, doing publishing and community work in a beard . . .
　　are we supposed to tell the Minister that he's just the sort
　　of chap this country needs? Does he say why he wants to be
　　British?
ARTHUR: Yes, because he's American.
BERNARD: Well he's got a point there.
　　Do you know America at all?
ARTHUR: Do I know America!
BERNARD: Americans are a very modern people, of course. They

59

are a very open people too. They wear their hearts on their sleeves. They don't stand on ceremony. They take people as they are. They make no distinction about a man's background, his parentage, his education. They say what they mean and there is a vivid muscularity about the way they say it. They admire everything about them without reserve or pretence of scholarship. They are always the first to put their hands in their pockets. They press you to visit them in their own home the moment they meet you, and are irrepressibly goodhumoured, ambitious, and brimming with self-confidence in any company. Apart from all that I've got nothing against them.

ARTHUR: My America!—my new-found-land! (*He takes surprising flight.*) Picture the scene as our great ship, with the blue riband of the Greyhound of the Deep fluttering from her mizzen, rounds the tolling bell of the Jersey buoy and with fifty thousand tons of steel plate smashes through the waters of Long Island Sound. Ahead of us is the golden span of the Brooklyn Bay Bridge, and on the starboard quarter the Statue of Liberty herself. Was it just poetic fancy which made us seem to see a glow shining from that torch held a thousand feet above our heads?—and to hear the words of the monumental goddess come softly across the water: 'Give me your tired, your poor, your huddled masses, the wretched refuse of your teeming shore . . .'? The lower decks are crowded with immigrants from every ghetto in the Continent of Europe, a multitude of tongues silenced now in the common language of joyful tears. (*By now* BERNARD *has fallen asleep.*) The men wave their straw hats. Shawled women hold up their babies, the newest Americans of all, destined, some of them, to become the captains and the kings of industrial empires, to invent the modern age in ramshackle workshops, to put a chicken into every pot, an automobile by every stoop, to organize crime as never before, and to fill the sky over Hollywood with a thousand stars! Nor is the promenade deck indifferent to the sight. Many a good hand is abandoned on the bridge tables, many a diamanté purse forgotten on the zebra-skin divans, as glasses are raised at the salon windows. New York! New York! It's a wonderful town! Already we can see the granite cliffs and towers of Manhattan, and Staten Island too, ablaze like jewels as a million windows give back the setting sun, and soon we have set foot on the New World.

The waterfront is seething with life. Here and there milling gangs of longshoremen scramble on the ground for the traditional dockets to work the piers, and occasionally two of them would give savage battle with their loading hooks. At the intersection of Wall Street with the Bowery the famous panhandlers, the wretched refuse of cheap barrooms, huddle in doorways wrapped in copies of the *Journal*. Behind us a body plummets to the ground—a famous millionaire, we later discover, now lying broken and hideously smashed among the miniscule fragments of his gold watch and the settling flurry of paper bonds bearing the promises of the Yonkers Silver Mining and Friendly Society. The air is alive with bells and sirens.

But now a new sound!—ghostly trumpets and trombones caught in the swirling eddies of the concrete canyons!—and a few more steps bring us to Broadway. Every way we turn excited crowds are thronging the electric marquees. Sailors on shore-leave are doing buck-and-wing dances in and out of the traffic, at times upon the very roofs of the yellow taxis bringing John Q. Public and his girl to see the sights of Baghdad-on-the-Subway. In threes and fours, sometimes in lines a hundred wide, the midshipmen strut and swing up the Great White Way chorusing the latest melodies to the friendly New Yorkers, to the dour Irish policeman swinging his night-stick on the corner, to the haughty hand-on-hip ladies of the night who have seen it all before. But it's time to tip our hats and turn aside, for the tall columned shadow of Grand Central Station falls across our path. We are booked on the Silver Chief.

Begging the pardon of a cheerful Redcap we are directed with a flashing smile to the Chattanooga train. Night is falling as we cross the Hudson. Friendships are struck, hipflasks are passed around, and cigar-smoke collects around the poker schools. A cheerful Redcap with a flashing smile fetches ice. The Silver Chief surges through the night. When we retire behind the curtain of our comfortable berths the roaring blackness outside the windows is complete, save for the occasional pillar of fire belching from the mines and mills of Pennsylvania.

And it is to fire that we awake; woods blazing in tangerine shades of burnt umber and old gold—the Fall has come to New England. The train drives relentlessly on, dividing whiteframe villages from their churches, and children from their hoops. And the woods give way to suburbs, and the suburbs to stockyards and slaughter houses, and the wind is slamming off the Great Lake as we pull round the Loop into Chicago—Chicago!—it's a wonderful town! Tight-lipped men in tight-buttoned overcoats and grey fedoras join the poker games. C-notes and G-notes raise the stakes. Shirt-sleeved newspapermen of the old school throw in their cards in disgust and spit tobacco juice upon the well-shined shoes of anyone reading a New York paper. A cheerful shoeshine boy with a flashing smile catches nickels and dimes as he crouches about his business. (*He crosses his legs, revealing Stars and Stripes socks.*) The air is scented with coffee and ham and eggs.

And the countryside is changing too as we swing south. Blue skies and grass are as one on the azure horizon of Kentucky. Soon thoroughbred stallions race the train on either side. Young girls in gingham dresses wave from whitewood fences. But again untamed nature overcomes the pastures—we climb through mountain ash and hickory into the Tennessee Hills. Tumbledown wooden shacks and rusty jalopies give no hint of life but the eye learns to pick out hillbilly groups sullenly looking up from their liquor jugs and washboards.

We doze and wake in thundery oppressive heat. Thick groves of oak and magnolia darken the windows of the speeding train—and encroach, too, upon the fly-blown shutters of white-porticoed mansions which stand decaying sill-high in jungle grasses that once were lawns. Atlanta is burning. A phlegmatic Redcap serves fried chicken and bottles of cherry soda. The poker players have departed. Big-bellied red-eyed men in white crumpled suits swig from medicine bottles of two-year-old sour mash bourbon. Enormous women in taffeta dresses stir the air with pan-handled fans advertising Dr. Pepper Cordials. The train bursts Alabama-bound into the blinding flatlands where cotton is king and a man and mule dominate a thousand acres of unfenced fields like a heroic sculpture. The sun hangs over them like a threat. Our wheels break into clattering echo as the iron girders of the Mississippi Bridge slash across the windows, sending shock-waves to make the glass pulse woomph-woomph around us. Far below, a boy on a raft looks up wistfully at the mournful howl of the Silver Chief, but that old green river rolls them along toward the bend where chanting Negroes heave on the rudder-poles of barges bringing pig-iron from Memphis and hogsheads from St. Louis—and where the last of the river boats working out of Natchez rides the oily waters like a painted castle way down yonder to New Orleans.

The train slows, crawling through the French quarter of the City on the Delta. The sun hangs like a copper pan over boarding houses with elaborately scrolled gingerbread eaves. In the red-lit shadow of wrought-iron balconies octaroon Loreleis sing their siren songs to shore-leave sailors, and sharp-suited pimps push open saloon doors, spilling light and ragtime to underscore the street cries of old men selling shrimp gumbo down on the levee. A dignified Redcap hums an eight-bar blues—how long, how long, has that evening train been gone?—At the back of the car a one-armed white man takes a battered cornet from inside his shirt and picks up the tune with pure and plangent notes. Soon the whole car—Bible salesmen, buck privates from Fort Dixie, majorettes from L.S.U., farm boys and a couple of nuns—is singing the blues in the night. (*He lights a cigarette—American brand.*) The sun drops into the smoke stacks of Galveston like a dirty dinner plate behind a sofa. The train picks up speed. When we retire behind the curtains of our comfortable berths the roaring blackness outside the windows is complete save for the occasional pillar of fire flaring up from oil wells under the cooling scrub.

BERNARD (*waking up*): Ever seen one of these before, Arthur?—I won this fiver off——

ARTHUR (*violently*): Ten thousand head of cattle on the hoof, packed together in a rolling river of hide and horn, meet our eye when we are woken with steak and eggs by a surly Redcap! The Silver Chief is on the Chisholm trail to Abilene! Amarillo—Laramie—El Paso—Dodge! The wheels roll, the rails curve, past the crude wooden crosses of Boot Hill where other lean-jawed men who once rode tall now lie in gunslingers' graves. (*He reveals a Sheriff's star on his waistcoat.*) And beyond, the open prairie. Tumbleweed races the train on either side. Lone riders whoop and wave their hats from lathering ponies and are lost to sight as we hit the dustbowls of Oklahoma! Where once the corn stood high as an elevator boy, and the barns shook with dancing farmhands changing partners to a fiddler's call, now screen doors bang endlessly in the wind which long ago covered up the tyre tracks of bone-rattling pick-ups taking the Okies on their tragic exodus to the promised lands of El Dorado. How easy now on the gleaming rails, now carving a path through the heart of the grain lands where the gigantic mantis-forms of harvesters trawl the golden ocean that fills the breadbaskets of America!

We climb with the sun out of the plains . . . Carson City —Sioux City—Tucson—Tulsa—Albuquerque—Acheson, Topeka and the Sante Fé—Wichita. . . . Snow-capped mountains shimmer on the horizon, and still we climb. From the observation platform at the rear we watch the shadows turn the thousand-foot walls of the Colorado River deep red and purple. Huddled in our blanket we sleep. Once we seem to wake to a nightmare of acrylic lights—against a magenta sky huge electric horseshoes, dice, roulette wheels and giant Amazons with tasselled breasts change colour atop marble citadels that would beggar Kubla Khan. But when the

cheerful Redcap shakes us all is peace. The Silver Chief is
rolling through vineyards and orchards, a sun-bathed
Canaan decked with peach and apricot, apples, plums,
citrus fruit and pomegranates, which grow to the very walls
of pink and yellow bungalows to the very edge of swimming
pools where near-naked goddesses with honey-brown skins
rub oil into their long downy limbs. Could this be paradise?
—or is it after all, purgatory?—for look!—there, where
picture palaces rise from the plain, searchlights and letters
of fire light up the sky, and a screaming hydra-headed mob
surges, fighting and weeping, around an unseen idol—golden
calf or Cadillac, we do not stop to see—for now beyond the
city, beyond America, beyond all, nothing lies before us but
an endless expanse of blue, flecked with cheerful whitecaps.
With wondering eyes we stare at the Pacific, and all of us
look at each other with a wild surmise—silent——
(*The door opens. Several men and a woman barge in as though
they owned the place, chatting among themselves.*)
I think you got the wrong room, buster.

DIRTY LINEN
concluded

*The room is occupied by two men, both Home Office Civil Servants, both formally dressed (*ARTHUR *and* BERNARD*).*

ARTHUR *has a file of papers among other paraphernalia.*

(*The door opens and in come* WITHENSHAW, COCKLEBURY-SMYTHE, MCTEAZLE, MRS. EBURY *and* CHAMBERLAIN, *chatting.* WITHENSHAW *goes to confront* ARTHUR *at the secretary/clerk's desk.*)

WITHENSHAW: What?

ARTHUR: I'm sorry—this is a Home Office Departmental Meeting.

WITHENSHAW: What are you doing here?

ARTHUR: We are meeting here for the convenience of the Home Secretary who has to answer the Division Bell.

WITHENSHAW: Well, I'm very sorry, but as you can see this room is occupied by a Select Committee.

ARTHUR: On the contrary, as you can see, it is occupied by a Home Office Departmental Meeting.

WITHENSHAW: Yes, but we were here first.

MCTEAZLE: Hello, Bernard—still soldiering on?

BERNARD (*standing up*): Mr. McTeazle, isn't it?—yes—yes—I was just showing young Arthur here—I bet you haven't seen one of these for a while (*produces £5 note*).

(*Meanwhile* WITHENSHAW *is writing another note for* MADDIE. *By this time* COCKLEBURY-SMYTHE, MCTEAZLE, CHAMBERLAIN *and* MRS. EBURY *have sat down. The* HOME SECRETARY *enters with a rush of words and sits in the Chairman's place.*)

HOME SECRETARY: Good afternoon, gentlemen—what a large gathering—difficult case?—I thought it was only that American—goodness me, let's keep things tidy can we? (*He starts stacking the mess of newspapers on the table.*) An

69

orderly table makes for an orderly meeting. (*He has the Mirror in his hands.*) Strewth!

Tit-tit-tut-tut-oh! (*Sees* WITHENSHAW *whilst folding the pin-up picture away.*) Hello Malcolm.

ARTHUR: This lady and these gentlemen are here for another meeting, Minister.

WITHENSHAW: Sorry, Reg, first come first served.

HOME SECRETARY: Are you Send-In-A-Gumboot?

WITHENSHAW: What?

HOME SECRETARY: Are you Rubber Goods Import Quota?

WITHENSHAW: No—no—we're Moral Standards in Public Life.

HOME SECRETARY: Oh yes, so you are—no hard information, I hear.

WITHENSHAW: We're not sure, Reg—something came up this afternoon.

HOME SECRETARY: Yes, well, I'm sorry to pull rank on you, Malcolm . . .

(*The Select Committee Members stand up;* ARTHUR *and* BERNARD *sit down.*)

. . . but I've got to deal with a very sensitive and difficult case——

(*The* HOME SECRETARY *picks up* WITHENSHAW's *note to* MADDIE, *who by this point has entered and is hanging up her coat.*)

What's this? 'Forget Claridges, the Olden Bottle . . .'

(WITHENSHAW *snatches it out of his hand and tears it into four and scatters the pieces.*)

MADDIE (*to* HOME SECRETARY): Hello, what are you doing here?

HOME SECRETARY: How do you do? My name's Jones. (*To* WITHENSHAW.) As I was saying you must have the room of course.

(ARTHUR *and* BERNARD *stand up,* WITHENSHAW *crosses to his Chairman's seat and the Select Committee sit down again. The* HOME SECRETARY *continues, the italicized words aside to* MADDIE.)

Noblesse oblige—say no more—anyway I'm expected at an Intrusion of Privacy Sub-Committee of the *Forget Le Coq au Vin and La Poule au Pot* Departmental Committee on Rag and Bone Men, Debt Collectors and Journalists.

ARTHUR: But Minister what about . . . ?

> (ARTHUR *holds out the folder. The* HOME SECRETARY *whips out
> a pen and signs with a flourish.*)

HOME SECRETARY: One more American can't make any difference.

> (BERNARD *approaches* WITHENSHAW *with the £5 note.*)

BERNARD: Mr. Withenshaw, isn't it? Take a look at this—there's
quite a story behind it——

> (WITHENSHAW *snatches the note and tears it into four pieces.*
> BERNARD *is crestfallen.*)

WITHENSHAW (*shouts*): Get out!

HOME SECRETARY: A word in your ear, Malcolm. Have you got
time for a drink?

> (*The Home Office men leave.*)

WITHENSHAW: Well . . .

> (FRENCH *enters and crosses to his place.*)

. . . not really Reg.

HOME SECRETARY: I'll give you a ring.

> (*The* HOME SECRETARY *leaves. An uncomfortable silence
> descends as the Select Committee settle down.*)

WITHENSHAW: Well now . . . where were we . . .

> (*Pause.*)

FRENCH: Mr. Chairman . . .

WITHENSHAW: Oh yes . . . you were about to make a point, Mr.
French.

FRENCH: Thank you Mr. Chairman. I have been giving this
matter a great deal of thought during our short adjournment.
I think I can say that never has the phrase *O tempora O
mores* come so readily to the lips.

COCKLEBURY-SMYTHE: Meaning what?

FRENCH: Meaning, 'Oh the times Oh the——'

COCKLEBURY-SMYTHE: I know what it means. Why was it on your
lips?

FRENCH: I am not a whited sepulchre, Mr. Chairman. I take no
pleasure in crying 'j'accuse'. But I have been talking to Miss
Gotobed. She has poured out her heart to me and I may say
it was a *mauvais quart d'heure* for the Mother of
Parliaments. Not since Dunkirk have so many people been
in the same boat—proportionately speaking. I am faced now

with a responsibility which I would dearly like to be without, but it seems I am presented with, to put it in plain English, a *fait accompli*. I have struggled with my conscience seeking an honourable course and not wishing to drag this noble institution through the mud.

WITHENSHAW: A very responsible attitude, Mr. French.

MCTEAZLE: ⎫
⎬ Hear, hear!
CHAMBERLAIN: ⎭

FRENCH: Thank you. I think I have indeed found a way. I propose we scrap the Chairman's Report as it stands and replace it with a new report of my own drafting. (*He holds up a piece of paper. He clears his throat and starts to read.*) Paragraph 1. In performing the duty entrusted to them your Committee took as their guiding principle that it is the just and proper expectation of every Member of Parliament, no less than for every citizen of this country, that what they choose to do in their own time, and with whom, is . . .

MADDIE (*prompting*): . . . between them and their conscience.

FRENCH (*simultaneously with* MADDIE): . . . conscience, provided they do not transgress the rights of others or the law of the land; and that this principle is not to be sacrificed to that Fleet Street stalking-horse masquerading as a sacred cow labelled 'The People's Right to Know'.

Your Committee found no evidence or even suggestion of laws broken or harm done, and thereby concludes that its business is hereby completed.

WITHENSHAW: Is that it?

FRENCH: It's the best I can do.

WITHENSHAW: How am I going to spin that out until Queen's Jubilee?

FRENCH: You can't. This is the last meeting of this Committee, unless you want to do it your way.

WITHENSHAW: No—no——

(MADDIE *throws her report and all her appendices in the waste-paper basket.*)

COCKLEBURY-SMYTHE: You'll have to get your peerage another way.

WITHENSHAW: The P.M. will kick my arse from here to Blackpool.

72

COCKLEBURY-SMYTHE: Services to sport.

MCTEAZLE: I would like to applaud Mr. French's understanding attitude and his stroke of diplomacy.

CHAMBERLAIN: Hear, hear.

MRS. EBURY: I move that Mr. French's report is put to the Committee.

COCKLEBURY-SMYTHE: Second.

WITHENSHAW: Have you got that, Miss Gotobed?

MADDIE: Yes, Malcolm.

WITHENSHAW: All in favour.

ALL: Aye.

WITHENSHAW: Against.

(*Silence.*)

FRENCH: Arsenal 5—Newcastle nil.

WITHENSHAW: Thank you, Mr. French.

FRENCH: Not at all, Mr. Chairman. (*He takes out his breast-pocket handkerchief, which is now the pair of knickers put on by* MADDIE *at the beginning, and wipes his brow.*) Toujours l'amour.

(*Big Ben chimes the quarter hour.*)

MADDIE: Finita La Commedia.

Dirty Linen was supposed to be a play to celebrate Ed Berman's British naturalization, but it went off in a different direction—*New-Found-Land* was then written to re-introduce the American Connection.

T.S.

Ed Berman, an expatriate American, founded Inter-Action, a charitable trust aiming to stimulate community involvement in the arts, in 1968. He now works as the Artistic Director of Inter-Action Productions (including the Ambiance Lunch-Hour Theatre Club, the Almost Free Theatre, the Fun Art Bus and the Dogg's Troupe). Not coincidentally like the American seeking British naturalization in *New-Found-Land* and like other members of Inter-Action's co-operative, he divides his time between the production company and work in schools, youth clubs, mental hospitals, community centres, playgrounds, remand homes and the streets. Most of his time is now spent as Programme Director of Inter-Action Trust, creating new community arts and action projects such as City Farms 1 in Kentish Town, and youth employment programmes. He still manages to direct some ten plays a year, mainly for children's and community theatre, and to perform in two hundred-odd shows. Ed Berman became a British subject on 5th April 1976, the date of the first public showing of *Dirty Linen* and *New-Found-Land*.